# PICTURE GANDHI

SANDHYA RAO

Tulika

For Amma, for everything. - S

**Picture Gandhi (English)**
ISBN 978-81-8146-376-0

First published in India, 2007
Reprinted in 2009, 2014, 2016, 2017, 2019

Design: Gowri Suresh

*Our thanks to Gandhi Smriti and Darshan Smriti for permission to access and use the photographs.*



Published by
Tulika Publishers, 305 Manickam Avenue, TTK Road, Alwarpet, Chennai 600 018, India
*email* reachus@tulikabooks.com *website* www.tulikabooks.com

Printed by
Sudarsan Graphics, Chennai, India

Once upon a time there was a man who lived a life so ordinary, he died without a paisa to his name. He was a man of peace who believed in the force of truth and love.

Once upon a time this man was a boy – a child like anybody else.

Gandhi was born in this house on 2 October 1869. It's a white house near the Arabian Sea in Porbandar, Gujarat. Many houses there are, or were, built with soft white stone. As a baby, he went all over the quiet little white town with his older sister or his nurse. He would not be alone because he was afraid of the dark.

These are photographs of Gandhi and his parents. He is seven years old here, and his family was now in Rajkot. What is he thinking about, looking so serious? Maybe he is thinking about how to bandage the guavas that have been pecked at by birds.

There are not many pictures of Gandhi as a child because there were not many cameras when Gandhi was a child!

Mahatma Gandhi's name was Mohandas Karamchand Gandhi. His mother called him Mohania.

Mohania was a very shy child and he was still afraid of the dark.

His mother's name was Putlibai. She was his father's fourth wife. A religious minded person, she was a follower of the Pranamis. They believed in both Hinduism and Islam.

His father, Karamchand, was not educated but he had a good job and his family lived comfortably.

Mohania didn't like going to school. He wanted to be with his mother all the time. Also, he was not very good at his studies, especially multiplication.

Gandhi wrote in his autobiography that he didn't remember much about his schooldays. But he did remember all the names they called the teachers!

How could Kastur go to the temple with my mother without asking me?

This is Kastur, Gandhi's wife. She is 16 in this photograph, and he is 14. They were both 13 when their parents got them married: Mohandas Karamchand Gandhi and Kastur Makhanji Kapadia.

He was very pleased to have someone to play with whenever he wanted to. He bullied her because he had been to school and she had not. He discovered that bullying her was no fun because she had a mind of her own and she often didn't care. She just did what she wanted.

Besides, Mohan was afraid of the dark and Kastur was not.

His father died in 1886, and in 1888, Kastur and he had a baby boy. They named him Harilal.

Gandhi had two half-sisters, one sister and two brothers. He was the youngest. Here you can see him, at 17, with his older brother Laxmidas.

After he finished school, he went to Samaldas College in Bhavnagar. But he didn't like it there. In five months, he was back in Rajkot with no idea of what to do next.

Why don't you go to England and study law, a family friend suggested.

It seemed like a good idea, and Gandhi was excited about going abroad. So, he packed his bags, said goodbye to Kastur and the baby, and got on a ship from Bombay – the city we now know as Mumbai.

On the ship he kept to himself. And he wrote. He recorded all that he felt, all that he saw, the people he met. He wrote with as much wonder about his first time in an English-style toilet as about the starry sky that seemed like a scattering of diamonds. After nearly 57 days, he reached England.

This is a London street about the time Gandhi lived in England.

Everything was different from home. Gandhi was still very shy and he had no friends.

So he tried to be like the others. He wore stylish clothes, learnt to eat with a knife and fork, and even tried to learn to dance and play the violin.

He was also hungry a lot of the time because he had promised his mother he wouldn't eat meat. Getting vegetarian food was difficult.

Here he is, sitting in front in a black suit, with members of the Vegetarian Society.

Yes, he managed to find vegetarians and a vegetarian restaurant called The Central! He even designed this logo for the Vegetarian Society.

He learned to cook simple meals for himself and ate only as much as he needed to.

He read books on philosophy and religion and studied as hard as he could. He found Latin very difficult but finally passed the law exams. He also did his matriculation and improved his English by reading newspapers daily.

He was now 21 years old and had been in England for three years. This is where he lived, just before he left England: at 52, Bayswater.

By the time he left, he had become a 'walker'. At first he did this to save the money he would spend on transport. Later, walking became part of his life and people scrambled to keep up with him.

When Gandhi returned to India he got a shock because his mother had died some months before. His family didn't tell him earlier because he was all alone in England. Who would comfort him there? Gandhi was heartbroken.

But he had a family to look after. So he went to Bombay, where he had decided to work as a lawyer. On his first day at the Bombay High Court, Gandhi found he couldn't speak in public. He was too scared.

He packed his bags and went back home to Rajkot. There his brothers found him some small jobs to do.

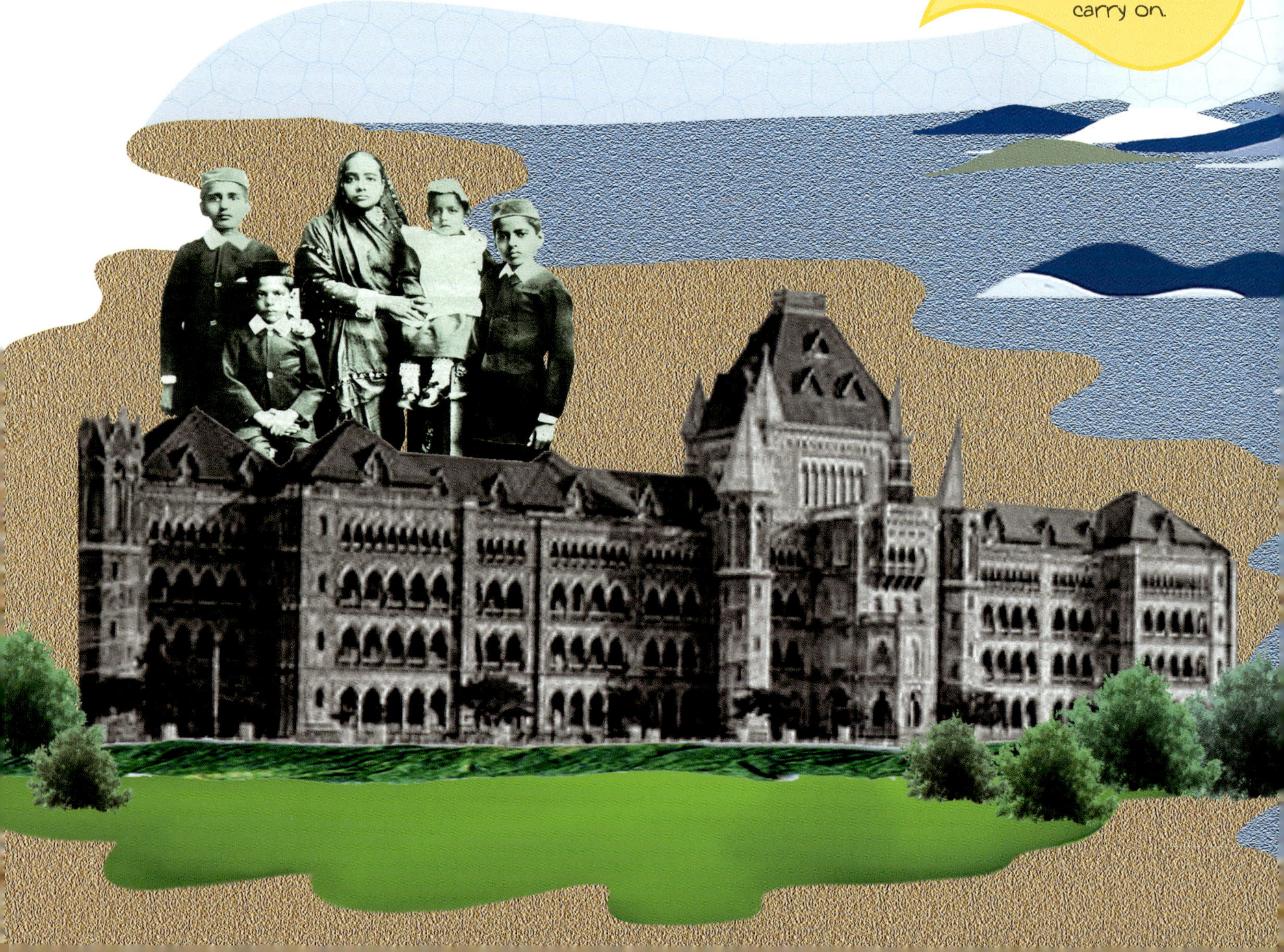

A few months went by. Then he heard that a businessman in South Africa was looking for a lawyer. The businessman's name was Dada Abdulla Sheth and he lived in Durban. He needed someone to work for him for about a year.

Gandhi decided to go, even though South Africa was far away. He wanted some way to escape the life he was leading in India, and this was the perfect opportunity.

It was April 1893. By now, he and Kastur had another little boy, Manilal. He left all of them behind and set sail once more.

He reached Durban at the end of May and went to work immediately, all dressed up as in this photograph, in a starched shirt, frock-coat and turban. He even wore patent leather boots, and looked quite different from how he looked in England.

When the judge saw him, the first thing he said was: Take off your turban!

It was a custom among Indians to cover the head, so Gandhi replied: I won't! And he walked out of the courtroom.

He wrote to the newspapers about this and the news spread.

About a week after he arrived in South Africa, Gandhi had to go to Pretoria. He had a first class ticket and took his place in the train.

The train moved. When it stopped at Pietermaritzburg, a policeman came in, dragged him out and threw him on the platform. You don't belong here, he said. I have a ticket, Gandhi said. I don't care, replied the policeman.

Sitting all alone in the dark and cold waiting room that night, Gandhi thought about the judge in the Durban court. He thought about how Indians were treated in South Africa. Why should people put me down because my skin is not white, he thought.

Sitting in the waiting room that night, he asked himself: Is this what I want? To be bullied? To be afraid? What is my duty?

That night he stopped being afraid of the dark.

From around the 1860s onward, many Indians were being brought to work on farms and in mines in South Africa. They had no freedom and no rights. They were treated like slaves.

After Gandhi completed Dada Abdulla's work, he decided to stay on in South Africa and do something to help the Indians there. Listening to Gandhi speak about their problems, they too grew bold. They helped him set up the Natal Indian Congress to fight for their rights.

Around that time came the news that Indians were going to be denied the vote in South Africa. Gandhi felt that the local Indians should fight this unfair move, and decided to stay back to organise the people. It was not going to be easy because Indians there were not exactly popular.

He opened his own office in Durban, so that he could earn a living as well as help people for free. The year was 1894. This is his team, along with some friends, posing in front of the office. He was now successful and fashionable!

Meanwhile, Kastur and two little boys waited for him in India. Kastur missed him. The boys hardly knew him. But Gandhi was working so hard, he could go and bring them over only in 1896.

By that time, Gandhi had become a well-known leader in South Africa. People in India too began to know his name.

D'you know this poem: 'Goosie Goosie Gandhi oh You never saw such a social Bore...?' This is what some locals thought of me!

There was a political organisation in India called the Indian National Congress, which was set up in 1885. People such as Gopalkrishna Gokhale, Balgangadhar Tilak, Surendranath Banerjea, Badruddin Tyabji, Pherozeshah Mehta, G. A. Natesan and others were part of it. Many of them met Gandhi when he came to India in 1896 and listened to his stories of South Africa.

Yet, when called upon to make a speech on one occasion, Gandhi's courage failed him and he could barely manage a whisper. Luckily, he had written down the speech, and someone read it out to the gathering.

Gandhi was particularly influenced by Gokhale who believed in Hindu-Muslim harmony.

In the short time that he was in India to take his family back with him to Durban, he printed and distributed a paper in which he wrote about the sad state of Indians in South Africa. Since the paper had a green cover, it was called The Green Pamphlet. News reporters sent information about the pamphlet back to South Africa. Unfortunately, they twisted the information and said things that had not even been written in it. These newspaper reports spread rumours in South Africa.

When the ship, the S. S. Courland, docked, an angry crowd was waiting in Durban harbour. Everything was quiet as Kastur and the boys got off.

But when Gandhi appeared, the crowd shouted: Surround him! Thrash him! They threw fish and rotten eggs at him and beat him with sticks and stones.

Luckily, Mrs R. C. Alexander, the wife of the police chief, was taking a walk nearby. She opened out her umbrella and stood between him and the crowd that was angrily chanting, "Hang old Gandhi on the sour apple tree!" The Alexanders somehow managed to help him get away on a ricksha.

Later, when he was questioned by police, Gandhi refused to say who had attacked him. He had come back this time even more determined to do what he needed for Indians in South Africa.

One day, a friend called Henry Polak gave Gandhi a book to read. It was *Unto This Last* by John Ruskin. Gandhi was so moved by it, he decided to live as Ruskin had suggested: in a group, working the land with their own hands, and doing everything themselves. This is how Gandhi and some others began to live in Phoenix Settlement near Durban.

Here they washed and cleaned everything themselves, even the toilets. They grew fruits and vegetables. They printed a newspaper. It was a simple life and Gandhi taught the children everything he knew and learned. Kasturba was a mother to everybody. They called her 'Ba'.

Life was hard, though. Ba saw how overworked her husband was, how troubled he was by problems. She also felt the burden of supporting him. Meanwhile, Ramdas was born in 1897 and Devdas in 1900. Gandhi had studied how to help at births. So he helped Kasturba give birth to Devdas.

A few years later, Gandhi's German friend, Hermann Kallenbach, gifted him a piece of land near Johannesburg. Gandhi made another settlement there and they named it Tolstoy Farm, after the great Russian writer Lev Tolstoy. Gandhi and Tolstoy admired each other and wrote to each other.

That's Kallenbach with Gandhi and his secretary Sonia Schlessin. This photograph has a story. Hermann Kallenbach loved this picture. When the First World War broke out in 1914, he folded this photograph tight and stitched it into the lining of his coat so that nobody could take it away from him.

The lines on the picture are the fold-marks!

Over the years, a series of unfair laws were passed which affected Indians living in South Africa. Gandhi complained to a minister, Gen. Jan Smuts, about these. Smuts said: Just do as I say now, and I'll make everything alright later.

Of course he didn't, and the terrible laws stayed. For instance, Indians had to give their fingerprints to the authorities, and only Christian marriages were recognised. Indians in South Africa were being put to all sorts of trouble. Something had to be done to stop this. Something strong.

No matter what, we did not stop publishing our paper, Indian Opinion.

Those days, Indians were not allowed to move about freely. For instance, they were not allowed to cross the border between Natal and Transvaal. Now, openly, thousands of men, women, even children, began to break the law by crossing the border. They had no permission to do so and no papers. They were led by Gandhi.

The police were not able to stop them from crossing, so they arrested them. Even Ba was arrested and put in jail for three months. Prisons overflowed, and still Indians continued to break the law and be arrested.

Finally, the British government of South Africa gave in – a little. That little was a huge victory.

Now, at last, Gandhi felt he was ready to return to India.

Thousands of people came to his farewell meetings – in Durban and Pretoria and Johannesburg and Cape Town. They called him 'Desabhakta Mahatma'.

In those days, there were no mikes. Gandhi did not have a powerful voice or manner. Yet when he spoke, the people listened. Even when they could not hear, they understood.

As Gandhi and Ba and the boys sailed across the waters, the First World War broke out. On board the ship, Gandhi began to learn Bangla. He had already learned quite a bit of Tamil and Urdu on earlier sea voyages!

After over 20 years in South Africa, the Gandhis returned home on 9 January 1915. A lot had changed in that time. The British had been in India since they first came as the East India Company in the 1600s. They were still there, and ruling.

Gandhi had been away too long. He asked Gopalkrishna Gokhale what he should do. Look for the real India, Gokhale suggested. So, Gandhi and Kasturba travelled, along with their dear English friend C. F. Andrews, all over the country. They went by train, in crowded third class compartments. They saw how ordinary people lived.

In the next 30 years or so, Gandhi made good use of the railways that had been built by the British for their own convenience. He went to faraway towns and villages, talking to people, urging them to forget their differences, be self-reliant, and join the freedom struggle.

He spoke with love and he looked like any one of them. When people heard that Gandhi was coming that way, they gathered in thousands just to see him or to hold their children up to him. If he was asleep, they woke him up. He didn't seem to mind.

Poor indigo farmers sought his help and he went all the way to Champaran, Bihar, to see for himself what their problems were. Mill workers of Ahmedabad, Gujarat, sought his help and he went on a fast to encourage them to continue their strike. From east and west, and everywhere, people came to Gandhi with their troubles and their tales.

With care and determination, Gandhi collected all the information he could. Then, after studying and checking the facts, he told them what to do.

One day, in September 1921, while he was in Madurai, he finally threw off his cap and his kurta. From that day on, he wore only a dhoti, the dress of a simple farmer. From that day on, the people of India knew they trusted him. He didn't only look like one of them. He lived like them, he understood them, he stood up for them. Most important, he listened to them, he believed them.

The leaders of the Indian National Congress, too, began to depend upon him. They looked to him for advice and to lead the way to freedom.

Quietly, firmly, he showed them how to live a life of simplicity and service, first from Sabarmati Ashram in Ahmedabad and then from Satyagraha Ashram in Wardha. He spun every day, and every evening he led group prayers. He wrote articles regularly and replied to letters immediately. He was strict with himself and with everybody else, those closest to him in particular. Maybe that's why once, many years later, when Bapu and Ba were travelling by train, Harilal met them at a passing station and gave his mother an orange. What about me, his father asked. No, not for you, Harilal replied, only for Ba.

Gandhi spoke with authority on behalf of the people of India to the most powerful leaders in the world. Sometimes people didn't understand what he said or why he said it. Sometimes he made mistakes. But at all times he believed that truth was god and at all times he looked for the truth, and spoke it.

He wrote it, too, in papers he published ever since his South Africa days. The articles he wrote in *Young India, Indian Opinion*, *Harijan* and *Navajivan* reached far and wide, and he often had debates with his readers through the letters columns.

All this meant he slept very little and this surely affected his health. But still he walked, still he fasted, still he worked, still he met with leaders and ordinary folk, still he led the fight for freedom from the British. He was gaunt and toothless with sticking out ears popping out on either side of a bald head, but his enchanting smile captivated everyone, particularly children.

Gandhi had a special relationship with children. In the ashrams, he happily took care of them while their mothers were busy.

It even seemed as though he was so busy taking care of everybody else, he did not have time for his own children. But by then he was Bapu, Father, to all of India. He belonged to everybody. And like all the other children in the ashrams in South Africa and India, his children too did what they could to help him. They too went to prison.

Even though India's freedom struggle was peaceful, thousands of people went to jail at different times. Ba used to be quite upset with Bapu that he was encouraging young men and women to go to prison!

The truth is, there were many who would do anything for him. Mahadev Desai, for instance. He was Gandhi's secretary for many years until he died in 1942. He and his family lived in the ashram with Bapu and Ba. They too lived simply and served, even if Mahadevbhai did not dress like Gandhi!

Then there was the tall and brave Khan Abdul Ghaffar Khan. He worked among the people of the North West Frontier Province and was known as 'Frontier Gandhi'.

There were many women and men who gave up everything to serve the country. They came because Bapu called.

Children, too, did little things children could do. They formed a Vaanar Sena, 'monkey brigade', in towns and villages, passed on information, collected donations, and spun on the takli, a small spinwheel.

Some of them even made sacrifices. Like M. N. Jois. He was returning from school one day when he saw bonfires on the main street. What is happening? he asked. We are burning foreign cloth, a man replied.

Those days, many people used to wear clothes made with cloth from England. Gandhi was urging Indians to use only Indian cloth – khaddar.

Immediately Jois took off his shirt and shorts and banian and threw them into the bonfire! When he got home wearing nearly nothing, his mother was not pleased. But how proud he was!

Most of all, Bapu had the support of Ba, close family and friends.

With them, in South Africa and in India, Gandhi showed how to stand up against injustice without killing or causing physical pain. He showed how to be ready to go to jail for what was right. And each time he thought someone had done something wrong, he punished himself for it by fasting.

When they saw Bapu suffer, people changed. Hindus and Muslims tried to come together, the British government became weak and gave in. Once, even his old enemy, Gen. Jan Smuts, sent him a telegram requesting him to end his fast!

In 1930, the British government unfairly attacked the poorest Indians by saying they had to pay tax on salt. Salt was the only flavour the poor could add to their food, and this too the British wanted to take away.

They cannot do this, Gandhi said. He thought hard until he came up with a plan that was so simple it was brilliant. He walked all the way from Ahmedabad to a tiny village called Dandi, about 385 km away on the Arabian Sea coast.

In Dandi, Gandhi picked up a lump of salt and showed it to the people gathered there.

In Dandi, cameras clicked. People cheered.

Then, all along India's long coastline, people began collecting salt and selling it. They were breaking the salt law. The police came to stop them but nobody fought back.

Newspapers and radios spread the news all over the world. Gandhi became a hero. Even in England, mill workers and common people cheered him and wanted to shake his hand when they saw him.

From 1939 to 1945, the world was in turmoil because of the Second World War. England was at the centre of the war. But India's freedom struggle still went on – quietly. Every day, Gandhi sat at his charkha, spinning. This was his way of praying for guidance and good sense. It helped him think of new and peaceful ways to break free from British rule.

Sadly, Ba died in 1944 when she and Gandhi were prisoners in the Aga Khan Palace, Pune. Just a few months earlier, Mahadev had died. And, even though Gandhi was surrounded by millions who loved him, he felt very, very alone. Ba and he had started their life together when they were both 13. Now they were nearly 75. Sixty-two years had gone by.

Meanwhile, the people were becoming restless. They could not wait any longer to be free. There was only one thing standing in their way: the cunning British policy of 'divide and rule' had led to a situation where it seemed as though the only way to freedom was by dividing India in two.

On the streets, in villages, towns and cities, Hindus began to kill Muslims and Muslims began to kill Hindus.

Gandhi tried to stop the fighting by fasting. This time, not everybody listened. Many Muslims packed up their bags and moved west to West Pakistan and east to East Pakistan. Hindus from there moved to India.

Finally, India and Pakistan became independent of Britain in August 1947. Muhammad Ali Jinnah became Qaid-e-Azam of Pakistan and Jawaharlal Nehru Prime Minister of India.

Many years later, East Pakistan became Bangladesh.

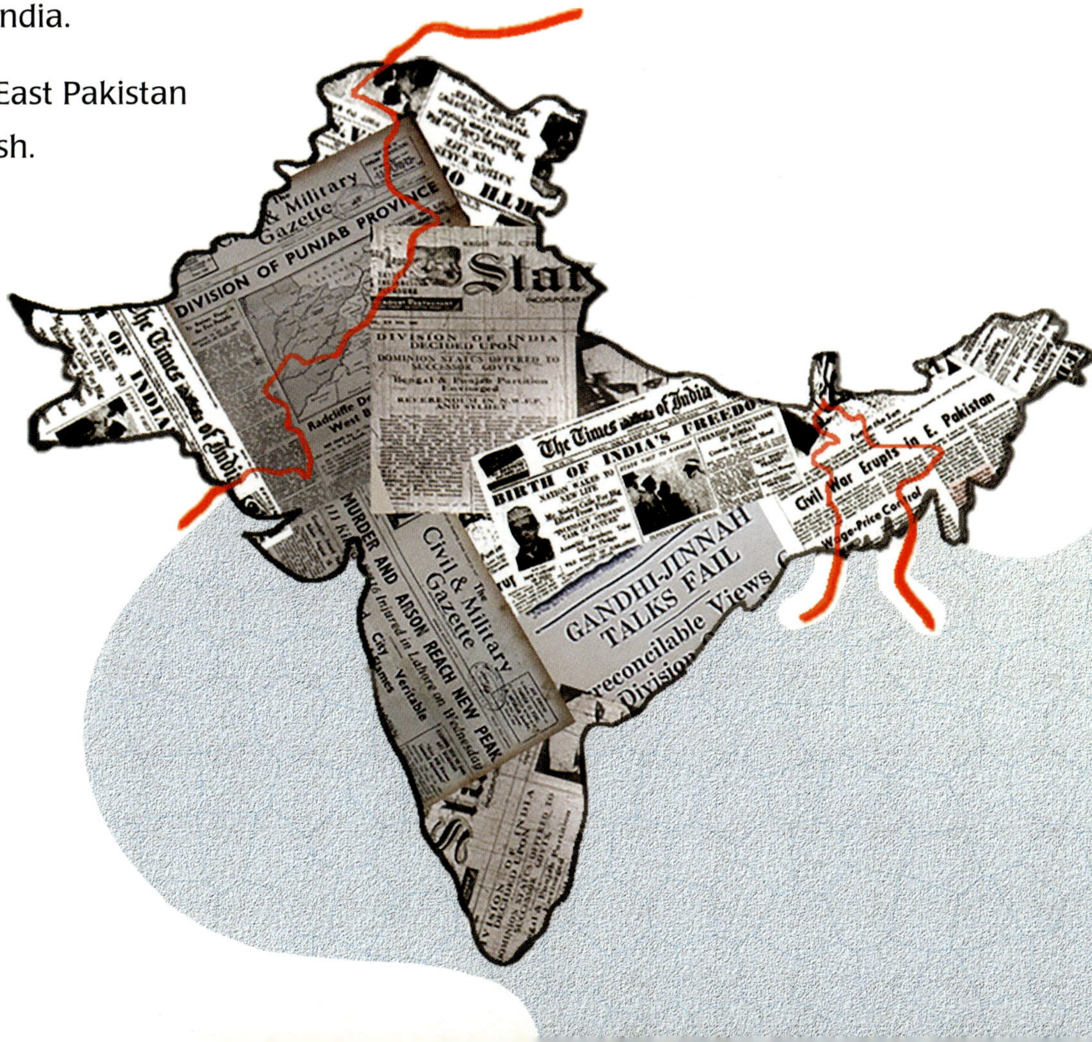

Gandhi had tried very hard but he was not able to prevent the division of India.

What would he do now?

There was one last thing. He picked up his stick and travelled to all the places where people were killed and were killing. Sometimes he was barefoot as he walked from house to house. Some people abused him. Some fell at his feet and wept. Everywhere, he stopped and listened and stayed the night in their homes.

As he comforted them with his presence and his prayers, he found it hard to bear the truth that India was divided. He felt that he had failed the people of India.

But the world remembers him as a man who showed how peace and love could win.

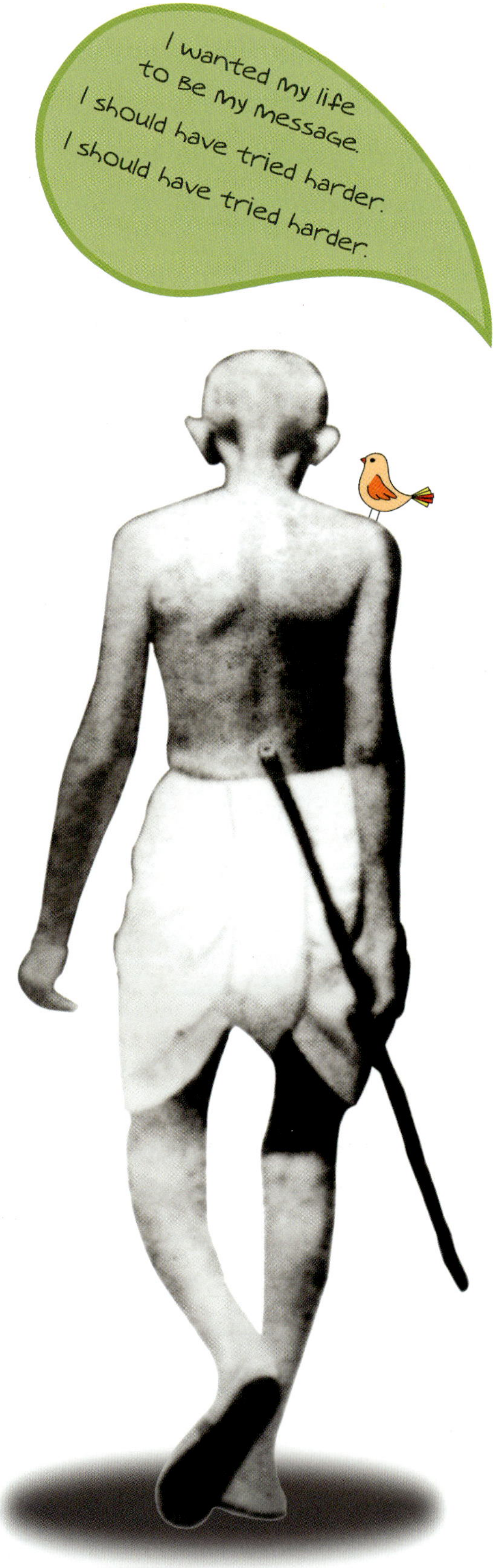

The story of his life has inspired people all over the world. Martin Luther King in the USA, Nelson Mandela in South Africa, the Dalai Lama who is the spiritual leader of Tibetans, Barack Obama, John Lennon, Albert Einstein, Aung San Suu Kyi... All of them have spoken of how much they learned from Mahatma Gandhi.

When he died on 30 January 1948, Gandhi was hurrying to evening prayers. He was late, and he hated to be late.

Once, long ago, he had grabbed someone's bicycle and raced to be on time for prayers. He had not ridden a bicycle for years!

This time, as he hurried to be on time, he got three bullets in his body and he fell to the ground.

There was a hush all across the nation.

How could this have happened? Why did it happen?

But the world knows that he showed the right way, and the world remembers.

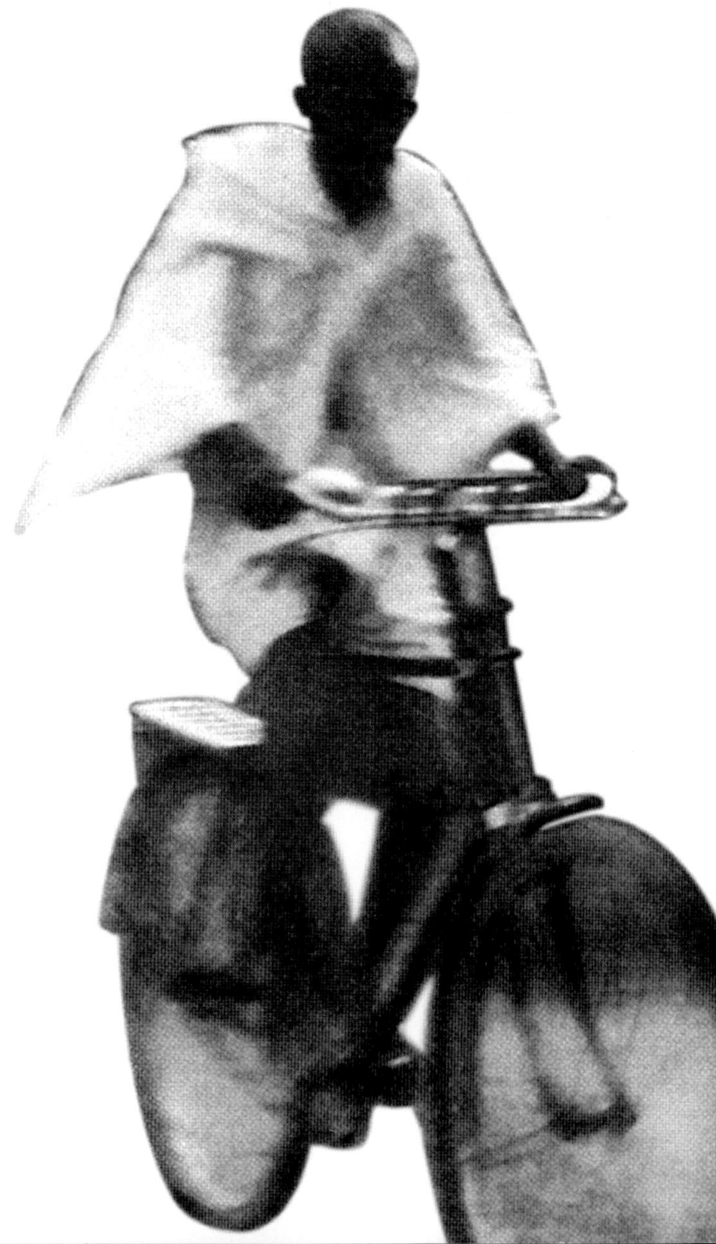

In his long life, Gandhi fought many battles against many people. Yet, he also formed deep friendships with the people he fought against.

For a while, Jan Smuts wore a pair of sandals that Gandhi had made for him when he was in a South African jail. When Gandhi first presented them to him, Smuts said he was not worthy to wear them.

Gandhi learned much from the British.

He had, after all, trained as a lawyer in England.

I love the English people, he said – it is their rule I oppose. And he walked with his hand on the shoulder of Lady Edwina Mountbatten, wife of the last British viceroy in India.

That is why his story will always be told. Because Gandhi showed that it is right to say 'No!' when something is wrong. He showed how to say 'No!' and still be friends.